Note to Parents and Teachers

The READING ABOUT: STARTERS series introduces key science vocabulary to young children while encouraging them to discover and understand the world around them. The series works as a set of graded readers in three levels.

LEVEL 2: BEGIN TO READ ALONE follows guidelines set out in the National Curriculum for Year 2 in schools. These books can be read alone or as part of guided or group reading. Each book has three sections:

• Information pages that introduce key words. These key words appear in bold for easy recognition on pages where the related science concepts are explained.
• A lively story that recalls this vocabulary and encourages children to use these words when they talk and write.
• A quiz and index ask children to look back and recall what they have read.

Questions for Further Investigation

I LIKE RED! explains key concepts about COLOURS. Here are some suggestions for further discussion linked to the questions on the information spreads:

p. 5 *What natural colours can you see around you?* Take children on a nature walk and encourage them to look for different coloured flowers, leaves, animals, skies etc.

p. 7 *What happens to some green leaves in the autumn?* They change colour from green to yellow, orange, purple or red. You could explain that some animals also change colour, e.g. foxes that change from brown to white, chameleons, salmon as they swim upstream.

p. 9 *What colours would you wear to hide in a forest?* e.g. greens and browns. Ask children what other animals use spots/stripes to help them hide e.g. zebras, tigers, leopards.

p. 13 *What colour is your hair? Is it a light or dark shade?* Ask children to think of other objects in different shades, e.g. shade of blue in water, clothes, green plants, face paints.

p. 15 *What colours are bright and easy to see?* e.g. red, orange, yellow. You could ask children who needs to wear bright colours, e.g. police officer, workers on building site.

p. 17 *What kind of weather makes a rainbow?* When the Sun shines on a rainy day.

p. 19 *Where have you seen coloured lights or filters?* e.g. lights on stage, disco lights, traffic lights. Ask children what coloured lights tell us, e.g. car lights/indicators, on/off switches.

p. 21 *What colours would you like for your bedroom?* Encourage children to do a drawing of their room, showing colours of different objects, e.g. bed, carpet, walls.

p. 23 *What colour might you be if you were feeling angry?* When people get angry they get red in the face, so we associate the colour red with anger.

ADVISORY TEAM

Educational Consultant
Andrea Bright – Science Co-ordinator, Trafalgar Junior School, Twickenham

Literacy Consultant
Jackie Holderness – former Senior Lecturer in Primary Education, Westminster Institute, Oxford Brookes University

Series Consultants
Anne Fussell – Early Years Teacher and University Tutor, Westminster Institute, Oxford Brookes University

David Fussell – C.Chem., FRSC

CONTENTS

4   **colour, natural, man-made**

6   **plant, flower**

8   **hide, camouflage**

10   **primary, mix**

12   **shade, light, dark, bright, dull**

14   **see, eyes**

16   **rainbow, split**

18   **glass, filter, lenses**

20   **dye, paint, chemical**

22   **mood, feel**

24   **Story: Let's Go on Holiday!**
A colourful holiday brochure
cheers up Sam on a grey day.

31   **Quiz**

32   **Index**

© Aladdin Books Ltd 2006

Designed and produced by
Aladdin Books Ltd
2/3 Fitzroy Mews
London W1T 6DF

First published in 2006
in Great Britain
by Franklin Watts
338 Euston Road
London NW1 3BH

Franklin Watts Australia
Hachette Children's Books
Level 17/207 Kent Street
Sydney NSW 2000

ISBN 978 07496 6847 1 (H'bk)
ISBN 978 07496 7028 3 (P'bk)

A catalogue record for this
book is available from the
British Library.
Dewey Classification: 535.6

Printed in Malaysia
All rights reserved

Editor/Designer: Jim Pipe
Series Design: Flick, Book
Design & Graphics

Thanks to:
The pupils of Trafalgar Infants
School, Twickenham, for
appearing as models in this book.

Photocredits:
*l-left, r-right, b-bottom, t-top,
c-centre, m-middle*
Cover tl, 2ml, 5tl, 8 both, 25tl,
26br, 27, 28bl, 29l, 30mr, 31ml
— Corbis. Cover tc & b, 2tl, 3,
7tr, 9, 10 both, 12tr, 13 both,
14-15 all, 16, 17t, 18, 19b,
20-21 all, 22 both, 24 both,
25br, 29r, 31tr, mr & bl —
istockphoto.com. 2bl, 28tl —
Photodisc. Cover tl, 4tr, 7b,
31br — Otto Rogge. 4b —
USDA. 5br, 30t & ml — Brand
X Pictures. 6b, 12bl, 31bc, 32
— Stockbyte. 12tl & br, 17br —
Ingram Publishing. 19tr — Marc
Arundale / Select Pictures.
23 both — Comstock. 26tr —
Flat Earth.

COLOUR

I Like Red!

By Sally Hewitt

Aladdin/Watts
London • Sydney

Everything you see around you has a **colour**. The sky is blue. Grass is green. Sunflowers are yellow. Earth is brown.

These are all **natural colours**.

This butterfly's wings are more than one colour.

Many things you wear and use are **coloured** with paints or dyes.

Many dyes and paints are **man-made colours**.

Blue dye

This girl's cotton shirt has been dyed purple.

Her bag is made of plastic. Its purple **colour** is **man-made**.

• What natural colours can you see around you?

Natural colours make the world look beautiful and interesting.

Plants come in many colours.

Plants use the green colour in their leaves to make food from sunlight.

Green plants

Colourful **flowers** attract birds and insects who visit them for food.

Birds and bees carry pollen from **flower** to **flower**. This helps new **flowers** to grow.

The colours of this toadstool warn animals that it is poisonous to eat.

• What happens to some green leaves in the autumn?

Colours that help an animal **hide** are called **camouflage**.

A cheetah has a brown spotted coat to help it **hide** in the long grass.

An arctic fox has a white coat to help it hide in the snow.

Cheetah

Macaws

Macaws live in a rainforest. Their bright colours help them to stay in a group.

In the bird world, bright colours help male birds attract female birds.

• What colours would you wear to hide in a forest?

Red, blue and yellow are called **primary** colours.

You can't make red, yellow and blue by **mixing** other colours.

All other colours are made by mixing **primary** colours together.

Primary colours

All these colours were made by mixing red, yellow and blue.

When you **mix primary** colours together in pairs, you make purple, orange and green.

Red and blue make purple.

Red and yellow make orange.

Yellow and blue make green.

Every colour comes in different **shades**.
Shades can be **light** or **dark**, **bright** or **dull**.

The apple is **dark** red.
The balloon is **light** red.

The tomato is **bright** red.
The brick is **dull** red.

Things can be sorted into colours. It is easy to spot all the red things and put them together.

It is harder to find things that are exactly the same **shade**.

This girl's face is painted in shades of brown.

• What colour is your hair? Is it a light or dark shade?

We **see** colours much better in the light than in the dark.

Our **eyes** can **see** colours, but some animal's **eyes** can't **see** colours very well.

Dogs **see** the world in black and white.

Cats see well in the dark. They hunt at night.

14

When we **see** colours, we are really **seeing** the colours of light.

So when we **see** a red flower, we are **seeing** red light bouncing off the flower into our **eyes**.

Light is made up of seven colours – red, orange, yellow, green, blue, indigo and violet.

Rainbow

A **rainbow** is a bow of light.

We see a **rainbow** when sunlight shines through raindrops.

The water **splits** light into seven colours.

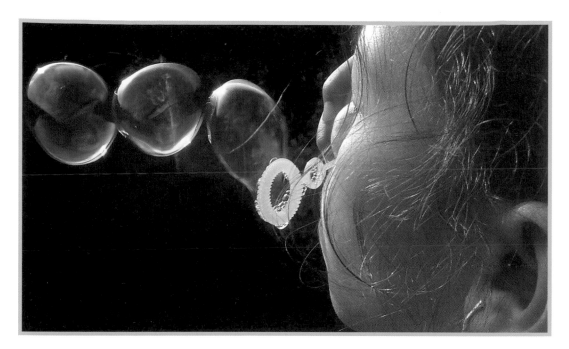

Bubbles

On a sunny day, you can see the light making **rainbows** in the skin of bubbles.

You can also see the colours of a **rainbow** when light shines onto the surface of a CD.

• What kind of weather makes a rainbow?

Stained glass

Stained **glass** windows are made of coloured **glass**.

Coloured **glass** is a **filter**. It only lets light its own colour shine through.

When light shines through coloured **glass**, the **glass** makes the light the same colour.

Sunglasses protect your eyes in bright sunlight.

Red **lenses** in the sunglasses are **filters**.

Red **glass** only lets red light through, so the world looks red.

Light shining through blue plastic looks blue.

• Where have you seen coloured lights or filters?

Dyes are used to colour things such as cloth, paint or hair.

Some natural **dyes** are made by boiling plants in water.

A dark blue **dye** comes from a plant called indigo. In the past, this was used to make jeans blue.

Blue jeans

Beetroot

Beetroot makes a dark red **dye**.

Onion skins make a brown **dye**.

20

Paint, wallpaper, curtains and carpets are coloured with **dyes** made with man-made **chemicals**.

You can choose from thousands of colours and shades when you decorate a room.

Pink bedroom

• What colours would you like for your bedroom?

Team shirts

Colours can tell us things.

Coloured shirts tell us
who plays for which team.

Colours can keep us safe.
A red light warns
us of danger!

22

We use colours to say what **mood** we are in.

- When we **feel** happy we are in the pink.

- When we **feel** jealous we are green with envy.

- When we **feel** sad we are blue.

• What colour might you be if you were feeling angry?

LET'S GO ON HOLIDAY!

Look out for words about colour.

It was a grey, rainy day. Sam and Millie were **feeling** in a gloomy **mood**.

"My friend Mike is going on holiday," sighed Sam. "I'm green with envy!"

"And I'm blue with cold!" shivered Millie.

"These will cheer you up," said Dad. He put some holiday brochures on the table.

There was a **brightly coloured** photo of sunny Jamaica!

"I want to go there," said Millie.

"I'd rather visit a jungle," said Sam.

"The **plants** are so many different **shades** of green," said Mum.

"What's that?" said Millie pointing at a photograph.

"It's a leopard," said Dad.
"The spots on its coat help it **hide** in the forest."

"I like the **bright lights** of a big city," said Mum.

"We could visit a museum or see **paintings** in a gallery," said Dad.

"And we could go shopping!" said Mum.

Millie and Sam groaned. How boring!

"OK," said Dad. "We could visit a fun park while we are there."

"Great!" said Sam. "Look at the **lights**," said Millie.

Millie picked up another brochure.
"Look at that **rainbow**," she said.
"That looks like the Victoria Falls,"
said Dad.

"But you will only see a **rainbow**
when the Sun shines," said Sam.
"You won't see one on a **dull** day like today."

"Let's go somewhere sunny," said Sam.

"We could go diving. I'd wear a mask so I could **see** all the fish."

"That starfish is so **brightly coloured** it doesn't look **natural**."

"It looks as if it has been **painted!**" said Dad.

"You can't **see colours** at the bottom of the sea. It's too **dark**," said Sam.

"What about skiing," said Dad.

"Why are they wearing **dark glasses**
in the winter?" asked Sam.

"The Sun is very **bright** in the white snow.
Dark lenses protect your **eyes**," said Dad.

"I want to go somewhere hot," said Mum.
"We want to go somewhere far away,"
said Sam and Millie.

Then Sam saw some pictures of children swimming, riding bicycles and having fun together.

"Let's go there!" said the children together.

"That's not very far away!" laughed Mum. "Never mind," said Millie, "It looks fun."

Use different **shades** of the same **colour** to **paint** a pattern. Then **hide** animals in the picture using the same **colours**.

Can you find **camouflaged** fish in this blue pattern?

QUIZ

What are the three **primary colours**?

Answer on page 10

Light is made up of seven **colours**. What are they?

Answer on page 16

What does the **colour** red tell you?

Answer on page 22

Can you remember what jobs these natural colours do?

Have you read this book? Well done! Do you remember these words? Look back and find out.

INDEX

B
bright 12

C
camouflage 8
chemical 20
colour 4

D
dark 12
dull 12
dye 20

E
eyes 14

F
feel 22
filter 18
flower 6

G
glass 18

H
hide 8

L
lenses 18
light 12

M
man-made 4
mix 10
mood 22

N
natural 4

P
paint 20
plant 6
primary 10

R
rainbow 16

S
see 14
shade 12
split 16